The Hungrumptious Blumpfh

and other poems

By Conrad Burdekin

Illustrations by Lilian Fitchett

Published by Olive Tree Books

First Published 2010
Second Edition

Olive Tree Books, Wakefield, UK.

Text ©2010 Conrad Burdekin
Illustrations ©2010 Lilian Fitchett

www.conradburdekin.com

Printed by
Beamreach Printing (www.beamreachuk.co.uk)

ISBN 978-0-9565863-0-8

To my Granny,

who would have
giggled like a girl at these poems.

Contents

Poetry is WOW!

Poetry is wow
Poetry is wild
Poetry releases
Your creative inner child

Poetry is whoosh
Poetry is bing
Poems flip your heart around
And make you want to sing

Poetry is great
Poetry is cool
Poems can be written
By any kid in school

Poetry is swish
Poetry is swash
Poetry is yummy food
For your brain to nosh

Poetry smiles
Poetry grins
Poetry laughs
And gives you feathered wings

Poetry is mega
Poetry is ace
Poetry is found
All over the place

Poetry should not
Cause you concern
Poetry is easy
It takes no time to learn

Don't wait any longer
Give poetry a go
Just use your pen to write some
And let the poems flow.

Sick Sid

"I'm sick," moaned Sid, "I can't go to school
Sending me there would be horribly cruel
I've got pains in my head and bumps on my back
My left leg is wobbly, my knees are both cracked.

A dirty great rash has spread over my toes
My hair's falling out and just look at my nose
It's covered in lumps and bright purple warts
My throat is so croaky I sound like a horse.

My belly's got spots on, my elbows are creaky
I'm falling apart mum, it's really quite freaky
My tongue is all twisted, my teeth have turned green
I must be the sickest boy you've ever seen."

"Off to the doctor," said mum, in a flash,
"He'll find the cause of the pains and the rash
He'll jab you and prod you and make you shout 'OW!'
He'll twist you and pinch you – come on, let's go now."

"Hang on, wait a minute," said Sid, "just a mo,
I think that my headache is starting to go
My legs are not wobbly, my knees have improved
My hair's growing back and my throat has been soothed.

The spots on my belly aren't there anymore
My back's not so bumpy, my head's not so sore
My tongue has been straightened, my elbows don't creak
The warts on my nose will be gone by next week.

I'm totally better, completely brand new,
Oh goodness, oh golly, oh whoop-a-de-do!"
"I knew it," growled mum, "I'm nobody's fool
Get into the car Sid, you're going to school."

My Homemade Stew

In my Homemade Stew I'll put...

Eye of toad
Ear of bat
Bubbling brains
Of a long dead cat
Tongue of newt
Sole of shoe
Wriggling cockroaches
Wormy goo
Hairs from the nose
Of an age old wizard
The freezing cold of a
Mighty blizzard
Lumps of mush
Slices of gunk
A scabby wart
From a creepy monk
Goblins' tears
A ghostly howl
Sharpened claws
Of a rat so foul
Graveyard soil
A skeleton's rattle

The deathly sound
Of an old hag's cackle

Here's my lovely Homemade Stew
Made by me – it's all for you!

Staying home with dad

The house is a tip
Mum's gone mad
She says it's down to me,
My brother and my dad.

The sofas don't have cushions
The table has no chairs
The wardrobes have been emptied
Our clothes are on the stairs.

The beds have lost their covers
The TV's kind of broke
The fireplace is fizzing
The lounge is full of smoke.

The budgie's gone, he's flown away,
Our cat has disappeared
Mum wants to know who'll find them
But no-one's volunteered.

The radiator's dripping
The freezer's lost its ice
The washer won't stop spinning
The lights have blacked out twice.

Mum's antique plate is smashed
Her perfume's on the floor
The front door key has snapped in two
But wait! There's even more:

The shower's fallen off the wall
The bath is full of beans
My sister's brand new silver tights
Have split along the seams.

The roof has lost its tiles
The car has been squashed flat
And though the budgie's come back home
We still can't find the cat.

Dad smiles and says, "Don't worry dear,
The boys and I had fun."
But judging by mum's stony face
I'd say our fun was done.

The Supermarket Crocodile

A Supermarket Crocodile
Saw me from the pizza aisle
He watched me for a good long while
Until I felt I ought to smile.

It didn't work
I couldn't do it
The crocodile grinned
He saw right through it.

Said croc: "I do like Pepperoni
Spicy beef and Mascarpone
But now I think you'll do instead
Come here, climb in, and mind your head."

"Not me," I cried, "I'm skinny and flat,
I'm bonier than an Egyptian cat
Twice as sour, a horrid taste
Munching me would be a waste.

Try this meat feast pizza, or,
This lovely veggie one before
You even think of eating me
I won't taste good, I'll spoil your tea."

"Won't taste good?" the crocodile said
Whilst salivating on my head
"Perhaps I need to have a try
I'll start by eating both your eyes."

Well that was that, I ran so fast
I didn't think my lungs would last
I ran until I turned pale white
I ran right through the day and night.

I ran past April, into May
I ran until my knees gave way
And then I ran another mile
To flee from Mr Crocodile.

He hasn't found me to this day
And therefore this is where I'll stay,
Hiding underneath my bed –
At least here I'm alive, not dead!

The Best Poem in the Universe, ever!

I've had a brilliant idea for a poem
It's great
It's wonderful
It's spectacular
It's fantastically amazing
It's the funniest, wackiest, cleverest idea I've
ever had
It's better than a school holiday
Stickier than treacle pudding
Sweeter than a sugar filled donut
Tastier than mum's chocolate cake
Scarier than a swamp monster
Buzzier than a bumble bee

It's…
It's…
It's…

gone.

Death Of A Mobile Phone

My mobile had a heart attack
The other day at school
Jimmy Wallace nicked it, then
He threw it in the pool.

I tried to reach it straight away
Whilst Jimmy stood nearby
But when my efforts didn't work
My phone began to cry.

It wobbled on the bright blue floor
And jumped up once or twice
But nothing I could do or say
Was going to save its life.

And then, just as it sighed its last
I heard a massive splash
Mr Jones, the swimming coach,
Had dived in in a flash.

He swam down to my mobile phone
And grabbed it in his hand
Then turned around and came back up
To put it on dry land.

"Quick, boy," he said, "come over here,
Don't stand around and stare
Get the water out the phone
And show it that you care."

I rushed around the slippery edge
Careful not to trip
But as I grabbed its watery shell
I heard my phone go 'blip.'

It coughed and spluttered for a while
I knew it must be ill
It sounded like a poorly frog
And then it just lay still.

I picked it up and dried it with
The towel around my hips
And then I tried the kiss of life
And smooched it on the lips.

I waited for a little while
And listened for a breath
I didn't want this sad event
To end with my phone's death.

Its keypad didn't seem too good
It turned a yucky green
The rest of it was looking worse
You should have seen the screen.

The battery melted in my hand
The sim card was destroyed
And when I looked at Jonesy's face
I got a bit annoyed.

"Couldn't you have saved my phone?"
I yelled in disbelief
But Mr Jones walked out the door
And left me with my grief.

So now I haven't got a phone
My mobile's in the bin
Although I did find Jimmy
And kicked him on the shin.

My Silly Daddy

I've got a silly daddy
He puts cornflakes in the kettle
And guess what he likes eating best –
A bowl of stinging nettles.

I've got a silly daddy
He wears trousers on his head
And just before he goes to work
He paints his eyebrows red.

I've got a silly daddy
He drinks mugs of margarine
And some days pours his cup of tea
Inside our washing machine.

I've got a silly daddy
He pats his car goodnight
He reads it bedtime stories
Then switches off the light.

I've got a silly daddy
He rides his bike up trees
And when we're at the seaside
He rides into the sea.

I've got a silly daddy
He hides under my bed
And when it's time for sleeping
He jumps onto my head.

I've got a silly daddy
I wouldn't swap him for the world
He's my silly daddy
And I'm his little girl.

Monster in My Bedroom

Watch out, there's a monster loose
Head of an ogre, body of a moose
Breath of a rubbish bin, snot of mouldy cheese
I'm behind the curtains, trying not to sneeze
Bedroom door creaks open, he sniffs and then he roars
Noisy as a sonic boom – as loud as when dad snores
Drooling on the carpet, he smells of rotten eggs
Creeping ever closer on elephant-sized legs
With blood red eyes he peers at me
Then rubs his giant tummy
I take a deep breath, open wide, and yell:
"I need you mummy!"
A click and then a high pitched scream
My room is bathed in light
The monster scarpers – disappears –
Into the dead of night
I search my room – he's really gone –
Then dive under my covers
Mum might have scared him this time round
But what if he's got brothers?

Doggy Poo

Watch out for that doggy poo
Splodge! Oh no, it's on your shoe
Spread along the corridor
All across the classroom floor
On the carpet, on the stairs
On the tables, on the chairs
Children hold their noses tight
Teacher shrieks, "Oh, what a sight!
Scrape off all that doggy muck
Get rid of that horrid yuck!"
What a stench, oh what a pong
People pointing all day long
Feeling bad you turn bright red
Wish that you had stayed in bed.

Little Sister

Little sister pushes her pram
She goes much faster than I can
She zooms like lightening round the park
She makes ducks quack, she makes dogs bark.

And when I try to make her stop
She starts to bawl and has a strop
She turns bright red and then goes blue
She's lost control, I'm telling you.

"What did you do?" says mum at home
"Can't you leave her well alone?
Look at her face, she's all upset."
"Just wait," I whisper, "I'm not done yet."

Mum goes, so now it's me and sister
I scowl down at the little blister
Time to get my own back sis
Sibling Revenge – oh what bliss.

My mind a-buzz with mum's complaints
I carefully reach for sister's paints
Quietly! Sssshhh! Take down the blue
Must not be seen by you know who.

Tip toe, soft step, shuffle shuffle, creep
Crouch down, wait, prepare to leap
Little sister does not have a clue
That soon she'll turn dark navy blue.

"Here I come!" and with a jump
I hurtle towards the annoying lump
But as I travel through the air
She turns, she ducks, then grabs my hair.

I miss her by a millimetre
"Geddoff!" I shout, "You little cheater.
My hair, let go, I'm telling mum."
She laughs and promptly bites my thumb.

I scream in pain as mum walks in
"Good grief," she cries, "what's all the din?"
"But mum," I moan, "it wasn't me
She bit my thumb – it's her, you see."

Mum doesn't see, mum doesn't laugh
Mum orders me to have a bath
Then straight to bed at half past five
A punishment for telling lies.

My gruesome, grotty sister's won
Yet again I've been outdone
I gnash my teeth and kick the bin
How come it's never me that wins?

No Clean Clothes

No clean shoes
No clean skirts
No clean trousers
No clean shirts.

No clean jumpers
No clean tops
No clean knickers
No clean socks.

No clean t-shirts
No clean clothes
Huge wet puddles
Lots of those.

"Don't jump in them
Wait! No! SPLASH!
Right, inside –
Clothes off fast."

Shivering, quaking
Chilled to the bone
No clean clothes
I'm being sent home.

Sweet Pete

A belly made of jelly
Ice-cream for a nose
Sticks of seaside rock for legs
Knees of pink marshmallows.

Face a yummy custard pie
Purple gobstopper eyes
Sticky sugared-donut mouth
And plenty more besides.

Lumpy apple crumble chin
Jammy dodger ears
Rows of crunchy iced-gem teeth
A sponge cake for his rear.

Hands of buttered hot cross buns
Chocolate logs for feet
Liquorice fingers, Starburst toes
Oh what a tasty treat!

King size Mars Bars for his arms
A fizzy lollipop tongue
Hair of yellow candyfloss
Shining like the sun.

I wonder what became of him,
What happened to Sweet Pete?
People said (and here I'm worried)
He looked good enough to eat.

Sprout Supporter

I'm a sprout supporter
I think everybody ought to
Eat a bowl of sprouts for lunch
Stinking, steaming, all should munch
Scrummy, yummy sprouts.

I'm a sprout supporter
I think everybody ought to
Scoff at least three sprouts a day
Boiled, fried, cooked any way
Squishy, squashy sprouts.

I'm a sprout supporter
I think everybody ought to
Make a sprout their bestest mate
Slap them on their dinner plate
Splendid, sumptuous sprouts.

The Hand in the Sand

I used to like the beach
I loved the sea and sand
That was, until last weekend,
Read on – you'll understand.

Mum was making sandwiches
Grandpa was asleep
Butch, our smelly mongrel dog,
Was curled up in a heap.

I went off to dig a hole
So I could bury dad
Despite the fact that mum had said
He'd probably go mad.

As I dug down in the sand
I felt a funny squish
Perhaps my spade had hit a crab,
A worm, or two dead fish?

What if I had found real treasure –
Jewels, a diamond ring?
I peered right in the deep, dark hole
But couldn't see a thing.

'Nothing for it, then,' I thought,
And plunged my arm in quick.
I knew if I found rotten fish
I'd likely be quite sick.

But no! My fingers curled around
An object hard and cold.
"Hurray!" I shouted to myself,
"I've found some pure gold."

I pulled and nothing happened
So I jerked and yanked and tugged
And as my breath was running out
The treasure came unplugged.

It shot out at the speed of light
I couldn't keep a hold
"Come back," I yelled, and turned around
To claim my precious gold.

But gold was not what I had found
No treasure in the sand
I'd only gone and dug up someone's
Real life human hand!

Its fingers were a deathly blue
Its fingernails were green
The thumb was twice as thick as mine
The knuckles looked quite mean.

Suddenly the hand woke up
It seemed to want a fight
It snarled and jumped onto my arm
And squeezed with all its might.

"Ouch," I cried and yelled to mum
To come and help me out
But she was much too far away
To hear me scream and shout.

By now the hand had scuttled up
My arm and clutched my neck
I couldn't breathe and gasped out loud
"It's got me. Help! Oh heck!"

The more it squeezed the more I thought
That I was going to die
The world turned deepest, darkest black
And stars blinked in my eyes.

"Wait," I heard a voice shout out,
"I'll get it with this chair."
A bash, a crash, a strangled scream
And – oh! Some lovely air.

My lungs filled up, I coughed and choked,
And spluttered for a bit.
"Don't worry, lad," the same voice said,
"That hand – I've dealt with it."

I opened both my eyes to see
A rosy cheeked old chap
Sitting in a deckchair with
The hand upon his lap.

"P-please," I cried, "get rid of it
That hand tried killing me."
"Of course," replied the pensioner
And flung it in the sea.

I ran back up the beach to mum
I couldn't wait to tell her
I'd just been saved from certain death
By a crazy old-aged fella.

"That's nice," said mum, "now how about
A tuna sandwich, dear?"
But I just kept on checking that
The coast was totally clear.

So next time if you're at the beach
And find a human hand
Run away as fast as poss
And leave it in the sand.

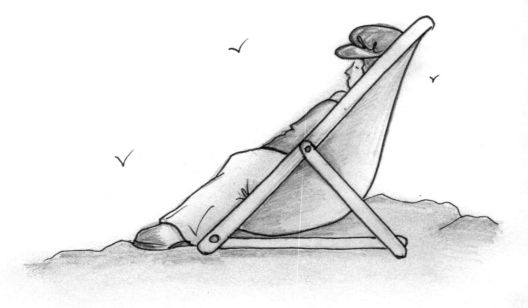

Important Questions

A garden
Is for gardening in
And a playground
Is for playing in.

A bath tub
Is for bathing in
And a shower
Is for showering in.

So why don't sinks
  s
    i
  n
   k
 ?

Or wardrobes
Have wars in?

Or drawers
Do drawings
And colouring in?

Down in the Dumps

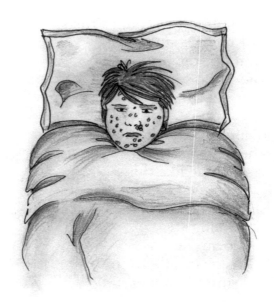

If you're feeling
Down
          in
   the
        dumps
If you're poorly or sick
Or in bed with the mumps
If you're scratching like mad
With the chicken pox
Had a bad day
Lost both your socks

If your homework's not done
And it's time for school
If your dad's coming home
Cos you broke all mum's rules
If last night you forgot
To put out the bin
If the world's in a mood
If you can't seem to win

No doubt you're depressed
So here's what to do
If something like this
Has happened to you
Listen up
Stop talking
Turn down the TV
It's time your attention
Got focussed on me

I know the secret
Of
    beating
            the
                dumps
I know what to do
When beset by the mumps
Chicken Pox
Lost socks
Homework to do
I have the solution
It's right here for you.

Are you listening?

Jump in the air
Climb a tall tree
Sing to the wind
Ask the clouds round for tea
Roll up a hill
Whizz down a slide
Squelch in the mud
Pinch your insides
Take photos of pigeons
Cuddle a bear
Swim with ten dolphins
Shave off your hair
Unwrap a present
Tell a worm your best joke
Spin round like mad till you
Fizz! like a coke
Splash in the sea
Pick your nose for an hour
Eat sixteen doughnuts
Then turn super-powered

And after you're done
If you're still feeling blue
I'm sorry, but really
What more can I do?

Sam's Space Adventure

Sam walked past school and instead
Tied a rocket to his head
Whizzed through Space to see the stars
Round the moon and over Mars
Zoomed a bit close to the sun
Burned his trousers and his bum
Sat down on the Milky Way
Tried to soothe the pain away
Felt much better, went to see
If he could find new galaxies
Did not see the black hole coming
School have had to call his mum in
"That boy will be the death of me
He'd better make it home for tea."

Will he?
You'll just have to wait and see.

45

Animals with Attitude

The jelly belly potamus
Climbed up onto our boatamus
That nearly was the endofus
Thanks to the jelly potamus.

The tufty flufty squirrel dit
Ran down a tree and squarely hit
My mother on the head a bit
It was, said dad, a tragedit.

The curly smelly piggle oink
Threw chocolate bars at baby boink
Then baby said to piggle oink
"Goo wada guffle biggle doink."

The coloured parrot rainbow flap
Made horrid gestures to a chap
And with his wing gave such a slap
The chap did not recoverap.

The sharply teethy crocobite
Is always looking for a fight
But when one came with all its might
The scaredy crocobite took flight.

A gentle kitten smitten puss
Made such a monumental fuss
When mum would not give tickleuss
That now she's in the doggy huss.

The fat old Kangaroo-do-bounce
Tried dieting and lost an ounce
He ate his food in small amounts
Said he: "My figure is what counts."

And what of porcu prickle pine
Who travels on the Northern Line?
He always gets a seat just fine
And reaches work at five to nine.

Unlike his friend the badger stripe
Who's always organising strikes
He's less use than a rusty pipe
That lazy snouty badger stripe.

Books

Books are like people
And people are like books
There's more to both
Than just their looks.

Some books are tall
Some books are small
Some books are wide
Some books are thin
Some books are funny
Some books are sad
Some books sound best
When they're read by your dad.

Books teach you stuff you might never have heard
About people and countries, in fact, the whole world
Books make you clever, books make you wise,
Books make you think, they open your eyes
Books are terrific, books are brill,
Books calm you down, they help you to chill.

You can read a book just about anywhere
At school or at home whilst you sit on the stairs
If your book's really good, you might even read on
When your mum says, "Lights out, it's bed time,
come on."
I find a torch is a good thing at night
After mum has switched off the big bedroom light.

A book is like having an extra best friend
A buddy on whom you can always depend
A book makes you happy when you're feeling ill
It's better than taking two headache pills.

So make today a book day – go on, be the first
To read a book, it'll quench your thirst
For fun, for laughter, for stimulation
It's more fun than playing on your Sony Playstation
Your X-Box, your Game Cube, Nintendo DS
Reading a book is quite simply the best.

My Mum

My mum goes to work in spotty bikinis
And sparkly high heeled shoes
Each day she gets up when the sun's still in bed
To decide on which clothes she should choose.

Her wardrobe is massive, it's tall, wide and long
It's got seventeen large purple doors
And under it, filled with a zillion shoes,
Are a hundred and two yellow drawers.

"I need them," says mum, when dad's in a huff,
"My shoes are my very best friends.
And as for my wigs and my long frilly coats,
I have to keep up with the trends."

Some mornings I've seen her waltz out through
the door
In pink slippers and lumo green tights
Last week she went shopping in nothing at all
My mum – no clothes – what a sight!

At weekends she wears lots of feathery hats
On Mondays it's silver string vests
Tuesday's her day for bright flowing scarves
But Friday's the day she likes best.

A Friday for mum means a ring on each finger
And two dangling out of her nose
Six from each ear and three in her lip
And ten more stuck to her toes.

The problem I have with her dress sense,
The thing that is not all that cool:
Mum is the acting headteacher
At my local junior school!

The Hungrumptious Blumpfh

The Hungrumptious Blumpfh of Munchton
Ate six snatchels whilst at school,
Drank four fozzbongs with a splashton
And then bellyscreamed, "More Food!"

Could no teacher stop his eat-yum,
Make him squidge a slightsome less?
Not a chance, oh not a gob-thong
Not for this strange gorge of mess.

Blumpfh devourfilled all his intakes
Chompled sixteen splugs for tea
Noshed a wholesome slice of fridgefull
Then declared, "Much more for me."

Blobbed his way up to the market
Chocolate crunched the whole lot there
Slobber scoffed the golden fudge blocks
Even tried to munch a chair.

But if you thought that would spellend
Blumpfh's junkunctual banquet race
Take a look above his shoulders
At his beetroot shiny face.

"Want more food," his jowly cheeks cried
"Must have now," his chindle dripped
"Won't stop till I've filled my greed bag,"
Squelched his over-active lips.

So he scoffed and ate and munchelled
Yes he gulped the whole day long
Though I'm sad to say at bedtime
Blumpfh exploded like a bomb.

Fish and Chips with Grandma

Every Friday after school
My Grandma fetches me
When I see her then I know
It's fish and chips for tea!

We always sit outside the shop
And eat tea on our knees
Even in the winter time
When all my fingers freeze.

Yesterday I ordered fish
And mushy peas with chips
But sadly all those tasty treats
Would never reach my lips.

I took my fish out of its bag
And said to Grandma, "Look."
Sticking out the fish's mouth
There was a rusty hook.

Grandma turned a shade of green
And jumped up off the chair
"You're not eating that," she yelled
"You really mustn't dare."

She grabbed the hook and lifted up
The fish for all to see
"Don't buy food from here," she yelled
Then threw away my tea.

I saw a blur of orange
Shooting past my head
Poor fishy landed in the road
And lay there looking dead.

A car drove right on top of him
And squished him to the floor
Grandma whispered in my ear
"That must've been quite sore."

By now my hunger had increased
I could have scoffed a horse
But all I had in front of me
Were chips and peas of course.

I scooped a pile of mushy greens
Onto my plastic fork
But then – would you believe it –
My peas began to talk.

"Hey kid," they said, "don't eat us,
We're really not so yummy
How about some tasty chips
To put inside your tummy?"

They carried on and tried to make
Me let them live a bit
But Grandma wasn't taken in
She wouldn't hear of it.

"Give me that fork," she said at once,
"Let's see if we've gone mad
I'm going to munch those mushy peas
You watch me, George my lad."

She got them up to her false teeth
In no time whatsoever
But then the peas began again
With cries of "No," and, "Never."

They started jumping off the fork
Like suicidal fleas
And soon a load of squishy green
Was covering my knees.

"Right," said Grandma, taking out
A huge white handkerchief
"Those peas are history, George my boy
This is beyond belief."

She grabbed them all without a thought
(I hoped they weren't still hot)
Then drew her arm back, said, "Watch this,"
And threw away the lot.

The hanky and the mushy peas
Flew high up in the sky
And when they landed on the ground
I heard them start to cry.

So now all that I had to eat
Were chips that had gone cold
And then I noticed one of them
Was growing yucky mould.

"That's not mould," my Grandma screeched
"It's yet another pea."
She picked it up and flicked it high
Into a nearby tree.

"Come on," said Grandma, getting up,
"Let's go elsewhere to eat.
Ice cold chips and talking peas
Are not much of a treat."

My Grandma says next Friday
It's tea at Pizza Hut
I just hope that all the food
Will keep its mouth tight shut.

What can I write about?

You can write about dogs
Chasing terrified cats
You can write about ducks
Wearing bright woolly hats

You can write about snakes
That rattle and hiss
You can write about cows
Eating packets of crisps

You can write about pirates
Sailing the seas
You can write about rainbows
Climbing up trees

You can write about tickling
A purple baboon
You can write about teachers
Who fly to the moon

You can write about mums
You can write about dads
You can write about grans
And wrinkly granddads

You can write about hamsters
With cute furry faces
You can write about doors
That lead to strange places

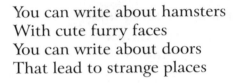

You can write about painting
A tortoise bright red
You can write about jumping
On top of your bed

You can write about houses
Full of pitch black
You can write about beanstalks
And young boys called Jack

You can write about pixies
With sharp pointy ears
You can write about princesses
Captured for years

You can write what you like
Just write till you're done
And make sure, most of all,
When you write, you have fun!

Sick

Lumps and bumps and sour chunks
Splats on carpets from top bunks
Yucky, smelly, horrid pong
Breakfast, lunch and tea gone wrong
Carrots, sprouts and grandma's dumplings
Feeling queasy, belly's rumbling
Acid burning in my throat
Taste of long dead farm yard goat
Nostrils full of red hot bile
Don't come near me for a while
Wish I'd never had that curry
Toilet quick, I'm in a hurry
Bathroom door locked, now there's trouble
Stomach vomit – feel it bubble
Rush down to the kitchen sink
Ghastly rotting cabbage stink
Stay there being sick for hours
Think I'm going to need six showers...

...at last, I'm done, I've been drained dry
Pale white face and blood shot eyes
Mouth of armpit, breath of pig
Hands all caked in dried up sick
Ringing ears and trembling fingers

Gruesome, awful smell still lingers
Tummy hissing, need to rest
No food thanks, I can't digest
Brain-ache mixed with poorly head
Crawl upstairs and into bed
See you in a week or two
(Unless, that is, I need the loo)

Disgusting Dave

Disgusting Dave refused to diet
Healthy food he would not try it
Bright green broccoli made him shiver
Water Melon made him quiver.

Tasty chicken salads, cool cucumber sticks
A single look at them, and Dave felt rather sick.
Crunchy orange carrots, leafy artichokes
Juicy red tomatoes – not for this huge bloke.

Disgusting Dave liked fatty burgers
Filled with globs of grease
Bacon butties – ten of those –
Topped with melted cheese.

Ice-cream for his breakfast,
Pizza for his lunch
Buttered popcorn, bags of sweets –
Munch! Munch! Munch!

Every day and every night
Dave ate and ate and ate
And when his tummy felt quite full
He'd put more on his plate.

Sticky Toffee pudding
Several chocolate cakes
Eighteen cans of fizzy coke
Oh how his stomach ached.

Chinese take-aways he scoffed
Followed by hot curries
Yellow custard pies for pud
With twenty six McFlurries.

Disgusting Dave went on and on,
Eating more and more
He grew so big, would you believe,
His tummy touched the floor.

But even then he shovelled down
More food into his belly
Deep fried Mars Bars, salty crisps,
Enormous wobbly jellies.

"You need to eat more healthily
You must learn how to slim
Stop eating such repulsive food!"
His friends all yelled at him.

Disgusting Dave refused to listen
Disgusting Dave refused to stop
Until – oh dear – last Thursday night,
His belly simply popped!

Her hair

I stood on a chair
To pull my sister's hair
After all, she's much
Taller than me

But sadly that's where
My reach for her hair
Ended –
She climbed up a tree.

Miserable Maurice
and Happy Horace

Said Miserable Maurice to Happy Horace:
"You're smiling like a clown."

Said Happy Horace to Miserable Maurice:
"It's better than a frown."

Said Miserable Maurice to Happy Horace:
"That grin is not the best."

Said Happy Horace to Miserable Maurice:
"Here, have some happiness."

Said Miserable Maurice to Happy Horace:
"It wouldn't work on me."

Said Happy Horace to Miserable Maurice:
"Of course it will, you'll see."

So Miserable Maurice gulped it down
And whaddya know – he lost his frown!

But did a smile appear instead?
'Fraid not – poor Maurice fell down dead.

(Happiness seems – for certain folk –
Much worse than death, and that's no joke.)

Pain in the...

My sister lies and fibs a lot
But if I tell my mum
She waits till no-one's looking
Then she kicks me up the...ouch!

That's the last poem
But don't shut the book
There's something else waiting
Turn over – have a look

About the Author

Conrad is tall, visits gazillions of schools across the whole of Yorkshire, and likes nothing better than making children laugh. He is a writer, storyteller and poet and lives in Wakefield with his wife, his three wonderful daughters, and rather too many slugs who love to slime their way through his office when he isn't looking.

To find out more about Conrad, please log on to www.conradburdekin.com where you can hear him read some of his poems and find out what he's been up to.

If you would like Conrad to come and work in your school, you can email him at:

conrad.burdekin@sky.com

This is his first collection of poems. He is so excited about it that he poured orange juice on his Weetabix this morning.

Conrad writing a poem in his office
whilst trying to avoid the slugs